I am a Cook Book

by **Em Riggs and Barbara Darpinian**
Illustrated by Martha Weston

Published by J. P. Tarcher, Inc.
Los Angeles
Distributed by St. Martin's Press
New York

Designed by The Amazing Life Games Co.
Production by The Committee

Printed in the United States of America.

Library of Congress Catalog Card No: 76-50965
Distributor's ISBN: 0-312-90606-4
Publisher's ISBN: 0-87477-067-X

Educational edition published by Learning Stuff, P. O. Box 4123, Modesto,
California, under the title of IT'S MORE THAN A COOKBOOK.

Trade edition published by J. P. Tarcher, Inc.
9110 Sunset Boulevard, Los Angeles, California 90069

Published simultaneously in Canada by Macmillan of Canada, 70 Bond Street,
Toronto, Canada M5B 1X3

1   2   3   4   5   6   7   8   9

My Table of Contents

A Note to Kids

Dear Kids:

Welcome to the d-e-l-i-c-i-o-u-s world of your own home cooking! With my help, you can become a super cook in no time, pleasing your friends and family with great snacks, sandwiches, and even breads and main dishes. I have 44 recipes of all kinds, and you probably won't need help from grownups to make almost all of them.

First look at the eight pages after the Note to Grownups. There I tell you how to measure, mix (without making too much mess), peel (and still have some carrot left), cut (the food, not yourself), and so on. Be sure to read Be Careful! on page 14, to keep from having accidents in the kitchen.

If you want to begin with the easier recipes, they are listed first in each section in my Table of Contents. To find out how many people the recipe serves, just count the little faces at the top of the page. (If you want to make a recipe for more or less than that number of people, that's one time you might ask a grownup to help you figure it out.)

Now get into that kitchen and start cooking. I only wish I were there to have one of your home-made meals.

Love,

I AM A COOK BOOK

A Note to Grownups

The pleasure of you and your kids (you can borrow someone else's if you don't have any) getting together to share in mixing, measuring, slicing, and peeling will be remembered for a long time. If the result is nice-looking and good-tasting food, great. If not, let the kids try again, when you're up to it.

Cooking can be satisfying to kids if grownups will share in a few of their flops and not boil over. An ounce of guidance and concern beats a pound of shoulds and ought-tos.

At the end of each recipe you will find a question. These are valuing activities designed to allow children to express feelings, reveal personal talents, focus on acceptance of self and others, and appreciate what others experience. These are suggestions for ways people can share experiences together. *I Am a Cook Book* is designed to bring big and little people together to share in the excitement of cooking and eating.

Doing It All

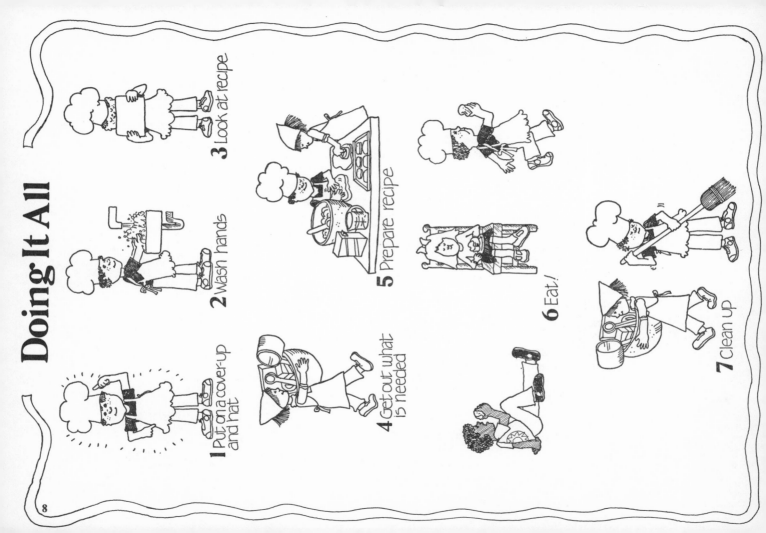

1 Put on a cover-up and hat

2 Wash hands

3 Look at recipe

4 Get out what is needed

5 Prepare recipe

6 Eat!

7 clean up

8

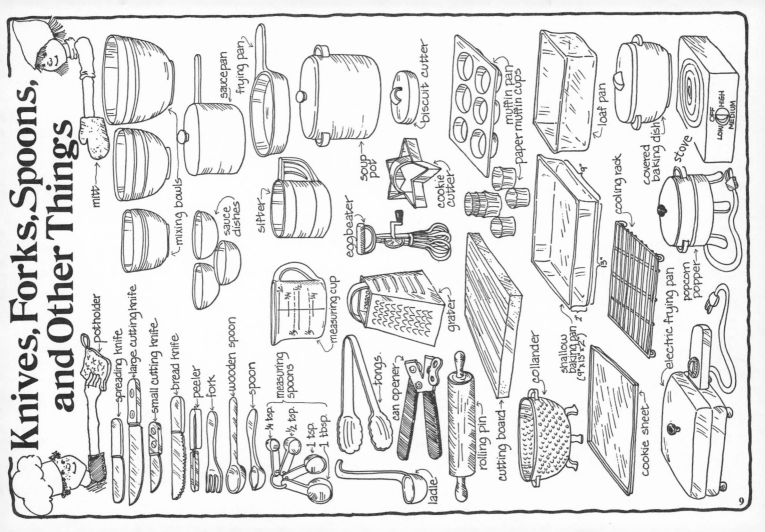

Knives, Forks, Spoons, and Other Things

mitt
potholder
spreading knife
large cutting knife
small cutting knife
bread knife
peeler
fork
wooden spoon
spoon
measuring spoons
¼ tsp.
½ tsp.
1 tsp.
1 tbsp.
ladle

mixing bowls
sauce dishes
saucepan
frying pan
sifter
measuring cup
tongs
can opener
rolling pin
cutting board
grater

soup pot
eggbeater
biscuit cutter
cookie cutter
muffin pan
paper muffin cups
collander
shallow baking pan (9"x13"x2)
cookie sheet

loaf pan
cooling rack
covered baking dish
stove
electric frying pan
popcorn popper

OFF LOW MEDIUM HIGH

9

Measuring Up

Measuring cups

1 cup

3/4
1/2
1/4

2/3
1/3

1 tablespoon (tbsp.)

1 teaspoon (tsp.)

1/2 tsp.

1/4 tsp.

Measuring spoons

Here's how to make a level spoonful.

1.

2.

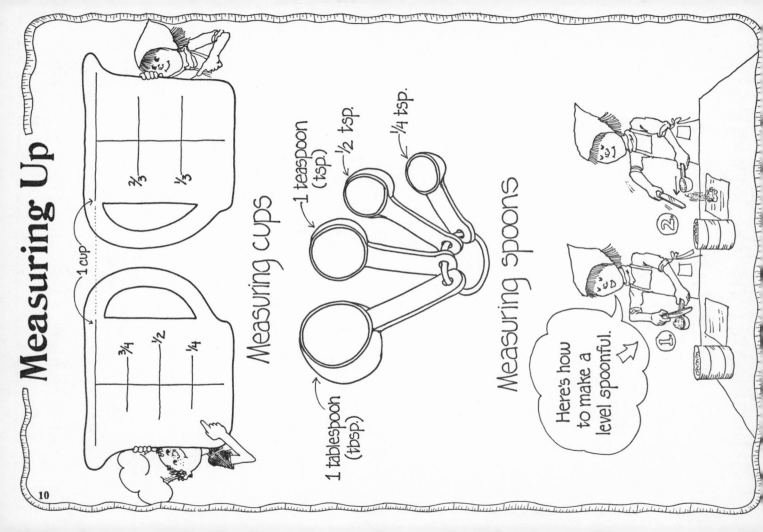

10

Break, Stuff, Spread

Break

Break in half

Break open

Break apart

Stuff

Stuff vegetables, or eggs, or turkeys.

Spread

11

Roll, Mix, Sift

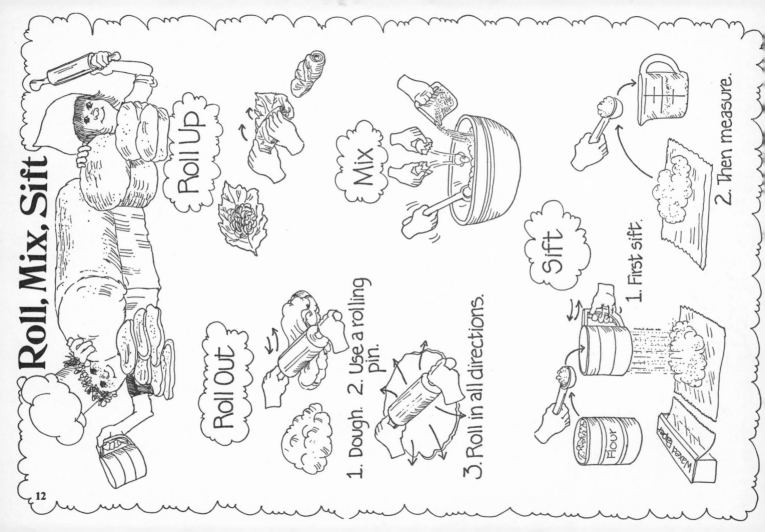

Roll Up

Roll Out
1. Dough. 2. Use a rolling pin.
3. Roll in all directions.

Mix

Sift
1. First sift.
2. Then measure.

12

Peel, Chop, Slice, Dice, Cut

Always carry a knife with the point down.

Always hold a knife by the handle.

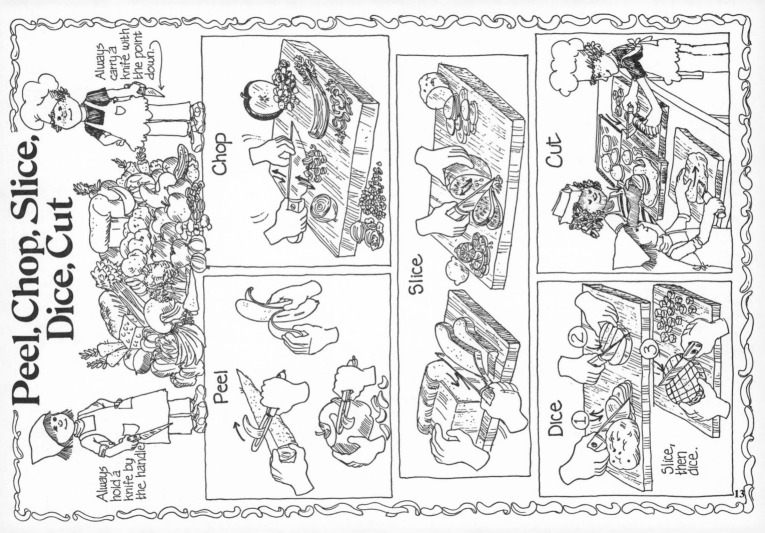

Chop

Peel

Slice

Dice

① ② ③

Slice, then dice.

Cut

Be Careful!

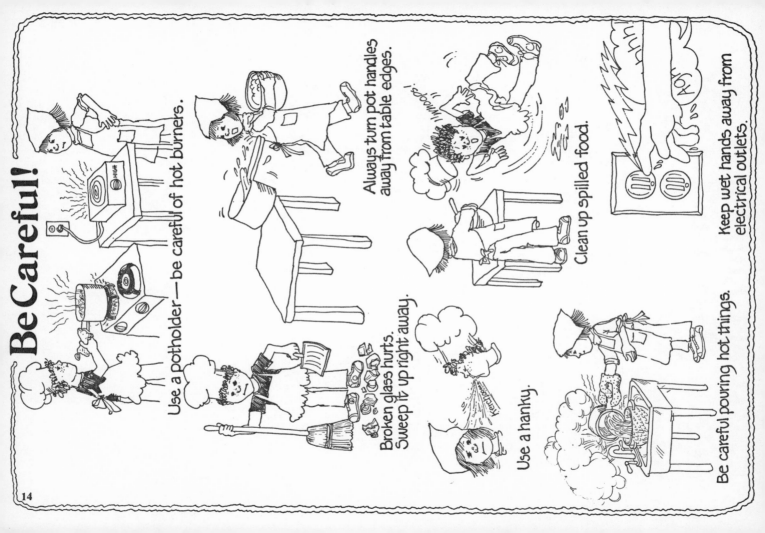

Use a potholder—be careful of hot burners.

Always turn pot handles away from table edges.

Clean up spilled food.

Keep wet hands away from electrical outlets.

Broken glass hurts. Sweep it up right away.

Use a hanky.

Be careful pouring hot things.

14

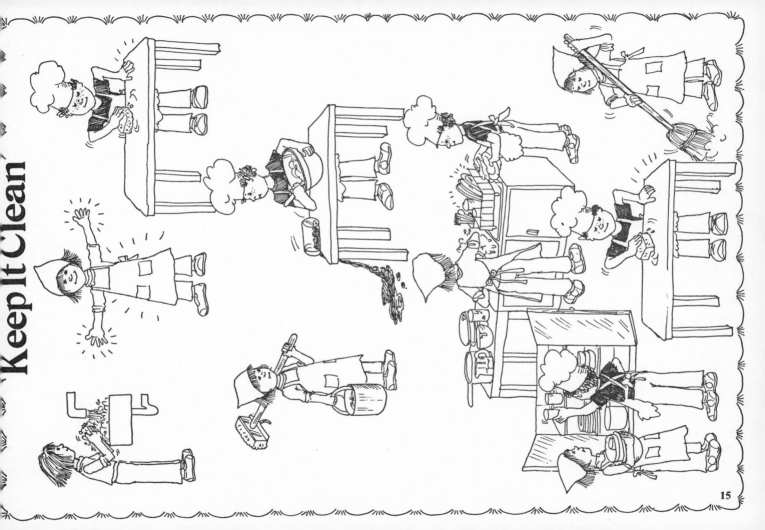

Keep It Clean

15

Hard-Cooked Eggs

serves ☺

WHAT I NEED

clean hands

saucepan

tong

1 egg

stove burner

water

sauce dish

Salt

salt

16

1. Put egg in saucepan. Cover with water.

2. Heat to boiling. HIGH

3. Reduce heat. Cook 20 minutes. LOW   20 min.

4. Turn off heat. Remove egg with tongs and put in sauce dish. OFF

5. Pour cold water over egg.

6. Shell egg when cool.

7. Eat with salt   CLEAN UP   Draw a picture of how you would decorate an egg.

17

SUNRISE SUPER SLUSH

WHAT I NEED

clean hands

wooden spoon

measuring cup

½ can water

Orange Juice ←½

½ c.→

MILK

½ cup milk

1 egg

5 paper cups

blender

6 oz.

Orange Juice

1 6 oz. can frozen orange juice

10 ice cubes

1 2 3

ICE CREAM VANILLA

3 scoops vanilla ice cream

18

1 Put milk, orange juice, ice and ice in blender. Blend 3 minutes.

2 Add ice cream. Blend 1 minute.

3 Pour into paper cups.

4 Drink!

CLEAN UP

Which do you think is best — instant foods or foods made from scratch? Why?

19

RIB-STICKIN' CEREAL

WHAT I NEED

clean hands

stove burner

wooden spoon

saucepan

potholders

sauce dishes

spoons

1c.

1c.

1c.

1c.

3 cups water

1c.

1/3 c.

1 1/3 cups oatmeal

Oatmeal

SALT

1/2 tsp.

1/2 tsp. salt

RAISINS

raisins

sugar

SUGAR

milk

MILK

20

1
Turn to medium. Put salt and water in pot.
1 c.
½ tsp.
SALT
1 c.
1 c.
MED.

2
1. Bring to a boil.   2. Stir in oats.
1 c.
⅓ c.
Oatmeal
MED.   MED.
3. Cook 5 minutes, stirring.
MED.
5 min.

3
Turn off and cover. Let stand 5 minutes.
OFF
Remove cereal
5 min.

4
Put cereal in bowls. Decorate with raisins.
RAISINS

5
Add sugar and milk. *EAT!*
CLEAN UP
SUGAR
What else can you make from oatmeal?

21

LIP SMACKIN' PANCAKES

WHAT I NEED

clean hands

2 mixing bowls

oil for pan

¼ cup melted margarine

1 cup white flour — White Flour

electric frying pan

spatula

wooden spoon

paper plates

forks

egg beater

syrup

1c. — 1 cup milk — MILK

¼c. ¼ cup orange juice

1 egg

½c. ½ cup granola — GRANOLA

½c. ½ cup whole wheat flour — Whole Wheat FLOUR

Honey — 1 tbsp.

SALT — ½ tsp. — ½ tsp. salt

Baking Powder — 1 tsp. — 1 tsp. baking powder

1 tbsp. honey

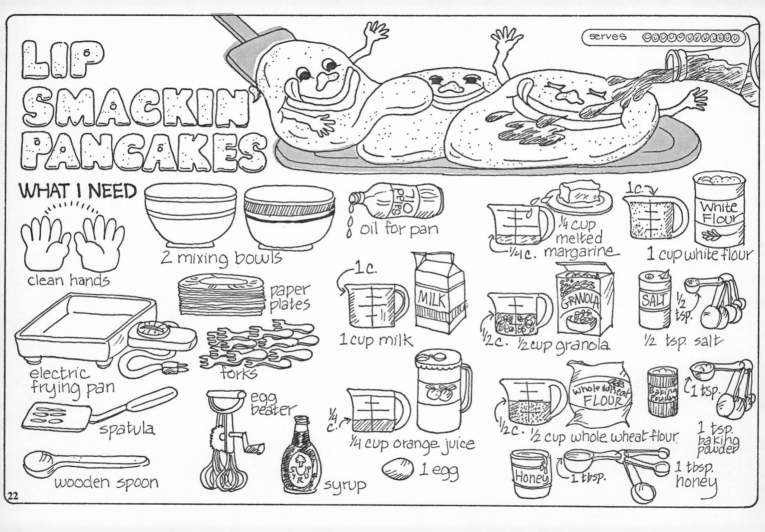

22

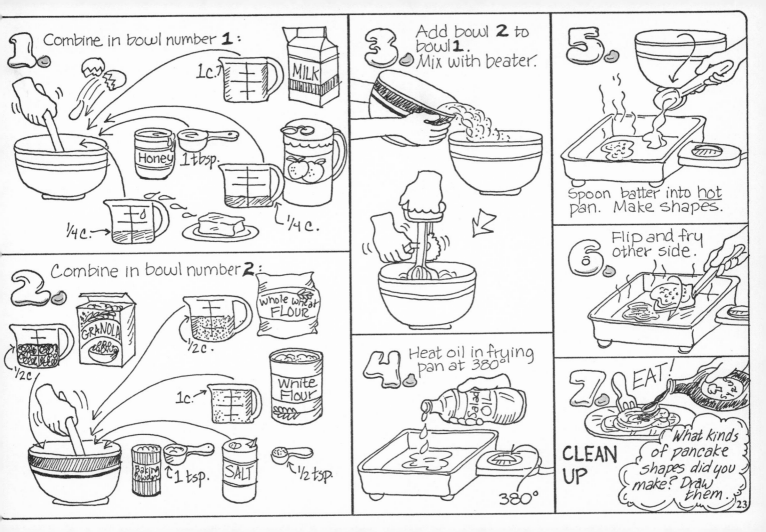

YOGURT SPOONSICLE

WHAT I NEED

clean hands

8 3oz. paper cups } 3oz.

blender

freezer

ladle

wooden spoons

1 6oz. can frozen grape juice } 6oz.

1 can water

1 8oz carton yogurt } 8oz.

24

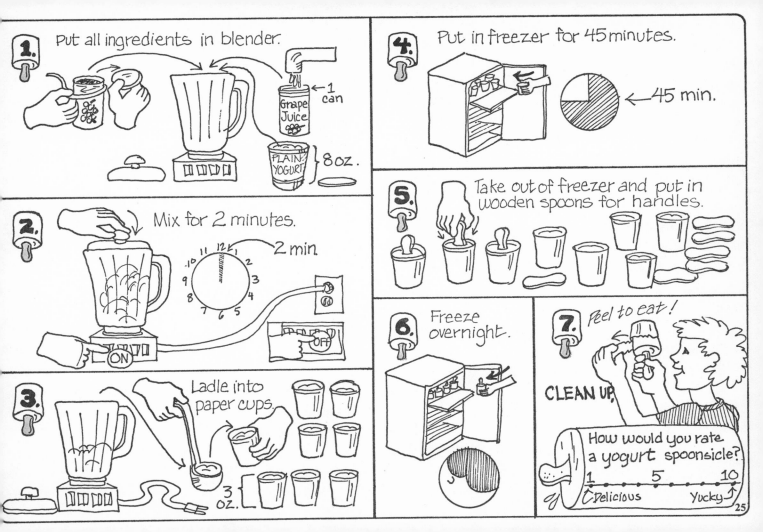

1. Put all ingredients in blender.
← 1 can
Grape Juice
PLAIN YOGURT } 8 oz.

2. Mix for 2 minutes.
2 min
ON
OFF

3. Ladle into paper cups.
3 oz.

4. Put in freezer for 45 minutes.
← 45 min.

5. Take out of freezer and put in wooden spoons for handles.

6. Freeze overnight.

7. Peel to eat!
CLEAN UP

How would you rate a yogurt spoonsicle?
1 Delicious   5   10 Yucky

25

Jiffy Jam

WHAT I NEED

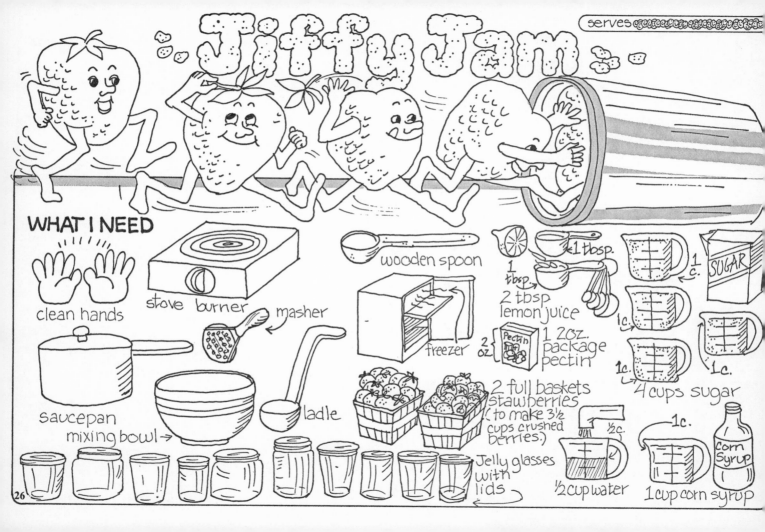

clean hands

stove   burner

masher

wooden spoon

freezer

1 tbsp.

1 tbsp.

2 tbsp. lemon juice

2 oz. Pectin

1 2oz. package pectin

SUGAR

1 c.

1 c.

1 c.

1 c.

4 cups sugar

saucepan
mixing bowl →

ladle

2 full baskets stawberries (to make 3½ cups crushed berries.)

Jelly glasses with lids

½ c.

½ cup water

1 c.

1 cup corn syrup

Corn Syrup

26

1. Wash and cap berries. Mash in bowl. Fill 3½ cups.

1c. 1c. 1c. ½c.

2. Add sugar and lemon. Mix.

1c. 1c. 1c. SUGAR 1c. 1 tbsp. 1 tbsp. 1c.

3. Combine pectin, water and corn syrup in pan. Turn to high.

2 oz ½ c. 1c. Corn Syrup HIGH

4. Bring to a boil, stirring constantly. Boil for 1 minute.

1 min.

5. Stir contents of saucepan into fruit mixture in bowl. Stir for 3 minutes.

3 min.

6. Cool to room temperature. Ladle into clean jars. Cover with tight lids.

¾ full

7. Freeze

CLEAN UP EAT!

What can you do in a jiffy?

27

1. Spread mayonnaise on bread.

2. Place cheese between bread.

3. Cut sandwich into 3 pieces.

4. Place on paper plate. Choose 2 friends to eat with you.

Pretend you are the cheese between the bread. How would you feel? Act it out.

CLEAN UP

29

Any-Kind-Of-Dog Sandwich

WHAT I NEED

clean hands

stove burner

saucepan

tongs

spreading knife

cutting knife

spoon

2 paper plates

water

1 hot dog bun

1 hot dog

catsup, mustard, relish

catsup   mustard   relish

1 Put hot dog in saucepan and cover with water.

2 Boil for 5 minutes.   Turn off stove.

5 min.

HIGH   OFF

3 Open hot dog bun.

4 Use tongs to put hot dog in bun.

5 Cut in half.   Put on paper plates.

Add mustard, catsup and relish.

6 Give your sandwich a name.

relish   mustard

CLEAN UP

31

CIRCUS SANDWICH

WHAT I NEED

clean hands

plastic fruit basket

peanut butter

1 animal cookie cutter

spreading knife

paper plate

3 slices bread

1

Make circus sandwich cage from plastic basket.

2

Cut 3 animal shapes from bread.

3

Spread peanut butter on 1 animal shape. Put another animal shape on top.

4

Spread on more peanut butter.

5

Put last animal shape on top.

6

Put on paper plate, upright.

7

Place circus sandwich inside cage you made.

CLEAN UP

Have a parade and show off your sandwiches.

33

Submarine Sandwich

WHAT I NEED

clean hands

spreading knife

cutting knife

paper plates

1 French roll

mustard

Mayonnaise

mayonnaise

Mustard

34

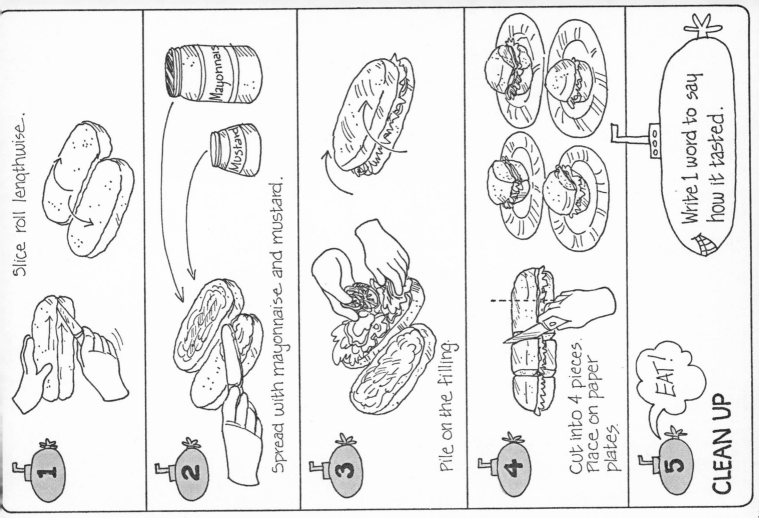

1 Slice roll lengthwise.

2 Spread with mayonnaise and mustard.

Mayonnaise

Mustard

3 Pile on the filling.

4 Cut into 4 pieces. Place on paper plates.

5 Write 1 word to say how it tasted.

EAT!

CLEAN UP

3

Fish-Wich Sandwich

WHAT I NEED

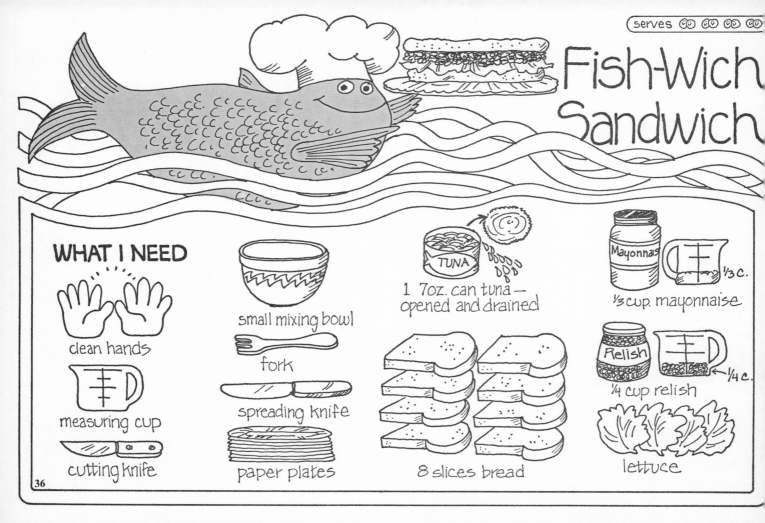

clean hands

measuring cup

cutting knife

small mixing bowl

fork

spreading knife

paper plates

1 7oz. can tuna— opened and drained

8 slices bread

⅓ cup mayonnaise

¼ cup relish

lettuce

36

1. Put tuna in bowl. Mash with a fork.

2. Add mayonnaise and relish. Stir.

Mayonnaise ⅓c.

Relish ¼c.

3. Spread filling on 1 slice of bread. Put lettuce on filling.

4. Cover with another slice of bread.

5. Cut sandwich in half. Place on paper plates.

6. Choose a friend to eat with you.

CLEAN UP

What kind of fish would you like to be?

37

SPROUT SAN

serves 1

WHAT I NEED

clean hands

small mixing bowl

fork

paper plate

spreading knife

chopped nuts

1 slice whole wheat bread

alfalfa SPROUTS

1 package sprouts

Cream Cheese — 1 tbsp.

1 tbsp. cream cheese

Mayonnaise — 1 tsp.

1 tsp. mayonnaise

38

① Cut bread in half.

② Mix cream cheese, mayonnaise and chopped nuts together in bowl with fork.

Cream Cheese

1 tbsp.

1 tsp.

Mayonnaise

③ Spread mixture on 1 bread half.

④ Sprinkle on some sprouts.

alfalfa SPROUTS

⑤ Cover with other bread half. Cut in half.

⑥ Place on paper plate.

⑦ EAT! CLEAN UP

Grow some sprouts. Keep a record of what happens.

39

serves 😊😊😊😊😊😊😊

ENERGY PUNCH

WHAT I NEED

clean hands

large mixing bowl

ladle

1 12 oz. can frozen juice

1 tray ice cubes

paper cups

3 cans water

berries   raisins   apple pieces   orange peel   banana bits   dried fruit (cut up)   cherries

1. Put water and juice in bowl.

2. Add fruit.

Dried Fruit

Raisins

3. Add ice to bowl.

4. Ladle into cups.

Drink!

Make up a T.V. commercial about this recipe.

CLEAN UP

Orange Juice

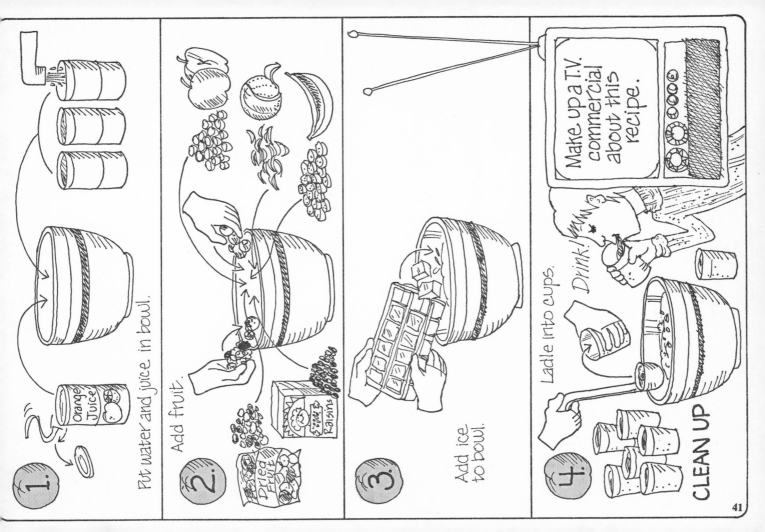

41

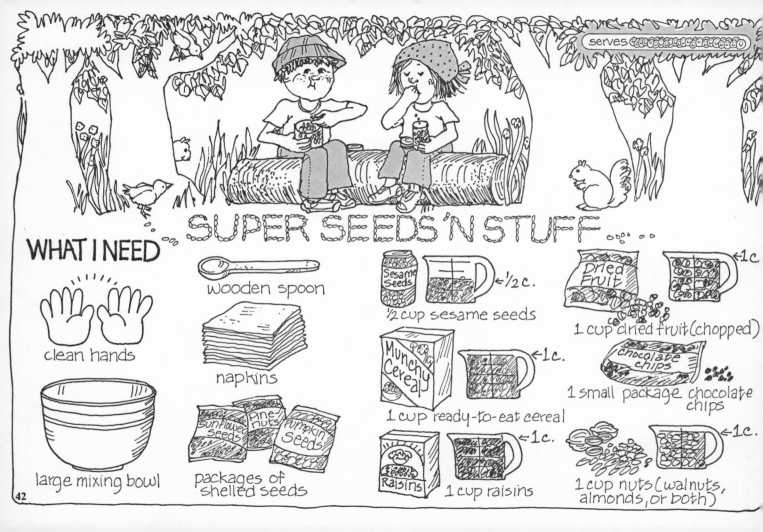

SUPER SEEDS 'N STUFF

WHAT I NEED

clean hands

large mixing bowl

wooden spoon

napkins

packages of shelled seeds

½ cup sesame seeds ←½c.

1 cup ready-to-eat cereal ←1c.

1 cup raisins ←1c.

1 cup dried fruit (chopped) ←1c

1 small package chocolate chips

1 cup nuts (walnuts, almonds, or both) ←1c.

42

1 Put everything in bowl — nuts, dried fruit, seeds, chocolate chips, sesame seeds, cereal, raisins.

1c. 1c. ½c. 1c. Munchy Cereal Raisins 1c.

2 Mix with wooden spoon.

3 Eat by handfuls.

CLEAN UP

Name other things that eat seeds besides people.

43

Tom Sawyer's Crunchy

serves

WHAT I NEED

clean hands

2 cookie sheets

wooden spoon

large mixing bowl

oven

jars

1 lb. box oatmeal

1 tsp. salt

1 tbsp. cinnamon

12 oz. jar wheat germ

3 oz. package coconut

1/2 cup nuts (chopped)

1/4 cup sesame seeds

1/4 cup sunflower seeds (shelled)

12 oz. jar honey

1/3 cup vegetable oil

1 tbsp. vanilla

1 350° Turn on oven to 350°.

2 Mix everything in the large bowl.

HONEY • Vanilla • 1 tbsp. • Coconut • Sun-Flower Seeds (Shelled) 1/4 c.

Sesame Seeds 1/4 c. • Cinnamon 1 tbsp. • 1 tsp. 2 • SALT

Vegetable OIL 1/3 c. • wheat germ • Oatmeal

3 Spread mixture on the 2 cookie sheets.

4 ←45 min. Bake 45 minutes.

5 Cool 10 minutes. 10 min.

6 Stir.

7 When cool, store in jars.

8 Eat like a snack.

CLEAN UP

What do you think children 100 years from now will eat as a snack?

45

serves

SILLY SOUP

WHAT I NEED

clean hands

wooden spoon

ladle

spoons

water

stove burner

soup pot

salt and pepper

soup bowls or sauce dishes

RICE

NOODLES

48

serves ☺

Walking Salad

WHAT I NEED

clean hands

measuring spoons

1 lettuce leaf

1 tbsp.

1 tbsp. cabbage (chopped)

paper towels

small mixing bowl

water

ice water

Mayonnaise

1 tsp.

1 tsp. mayonnaise

fork

salt and pepper

1. Wash lettuce.

2. Put lettuce in ice water. (count to 100)

123456789
1011121314 15 16
17 18 19 20 21 22 23
24 25 26 27 28 29
30 31 32 33 34 35
36 37 38 39 40 41
42 43 44 45 46 47 48
49 50 51 52 53 54 55
56 57 58 59 60 61 62 63
64 65 66 67 68 69 70 71 72 73
74 75 76 77 78 79 80 81 82 83
84 85 86 87 88 89 90 91 92
93 94 95 96 97 98 99 100 !

3. Pat lettuce dry with paper towels.

4. Mix mayonnaise with chopped cabbage in bowl.

1 tbsp.
1 tsp.
Mayonnaise

5. Place cabbage on center of lettuce. Add salt and pepper.

P
S

6. Roll like a cone. Walk around and eat it.

CLEAN UP   What other kinds of foods can you take for a walk?

5

DEVILED EGG SALAD

WHAT I NEED

clean hands

measuring spoons

spoon

sauce dish

fork

2 paper plates

cutting knife

1 hard-boiled egg

Mayonnaise

1 tsp. mayonnaise

salt, pepper   paprika

Relish
1 tsp.
1 tsp. relish

Mustard
½ tsp.
½ tsp. mustard

2 green vegetable leaves

① Shell egg.

② Cut egg in half lengthwise.

③ Put yolk in sauce dish. Mash with fork.

④ Relish ⊤ 1 tsp.
Mustard ⊤ ½ tsp.
1 tsp.
Mayonnaise
Add salt, pepper, mustard, relish and mayonnaise. Mix.

⑤ Use spoon to fill each egg half.
Sprinkle paprika over top.

⑥ Place green vegetable leaves on plates. Put egg halves on top.

⑦ EAT!
CLEAN UP

How do you act when you feel devilish?

53

Banana Split Salad

WHAT I NEED

clean hands

cutting knife

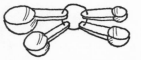
measuring spoons

4 paper plates

4 forks

1 banana

small can fruit cocktail (opened)

4 lettuce leaves

nuts (chopped)

1 tsp.
1 tsp.
1 tsp.
1 tsp.
4 tsps. cottage cheese

dried fruit

54

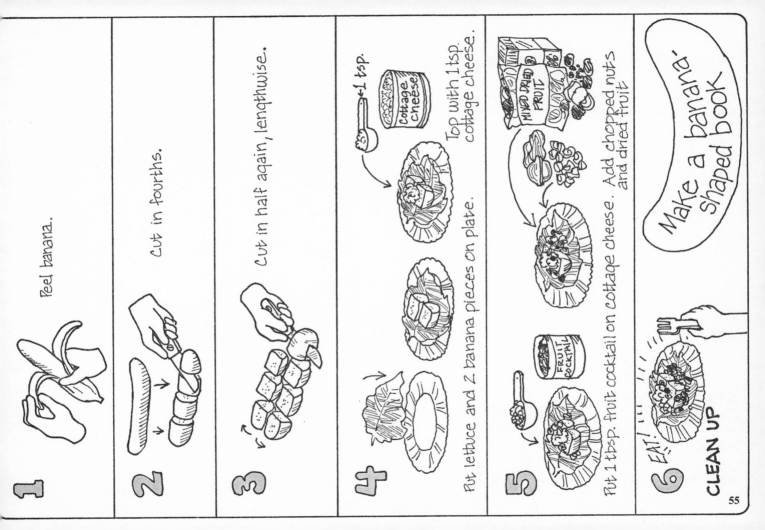

1 Peel banana.

2 Cut in fourths.

3 Cut in half again, lengthwise.

4 Put lettuce and 2 banana pieces on plate.

Top with 1 tsp. cottage cheese.

←1 tsp.

Cottage cheese

5 Put 1 tbsp. fruit cocktail on cottage cheese. Add chopped nuts and dried fruit

MIXED DRIED FRUIT

FRUIT COCKTAIL

6 *EAT!*

CLEAN UP

Make a banana-shaped book

55

Jiggly Gelatin Salad

serves 🙂🙂🙂🙂🙂🙂

WHAT I NEED

clean hands

muffin pan

6 spoons

½ package flavored gelatin

stove burner

6 paper muffin cups

grater

carrot

wooden spoon

saucepan

refrigerator

½ cup water ←½ cup

½→ cup ½ cup fruit juice

1. Heat water to boiling. ½ c.

2. Turn off heat. Add gelatin. Stir. Add fruit juice. Stir.

3. Grate ½ of carrot.

4. Add grated carrot to gelatin mixture.

5. Put paper baking cups in muffin pan. Pour gelatin into baking cups.

6. Refrigerate overnight.

7. EAT TOMORROW. CLEAN UP. If you could be a jiggly gelatin, what kind would you be?

57

APPLES 'N NUTTER

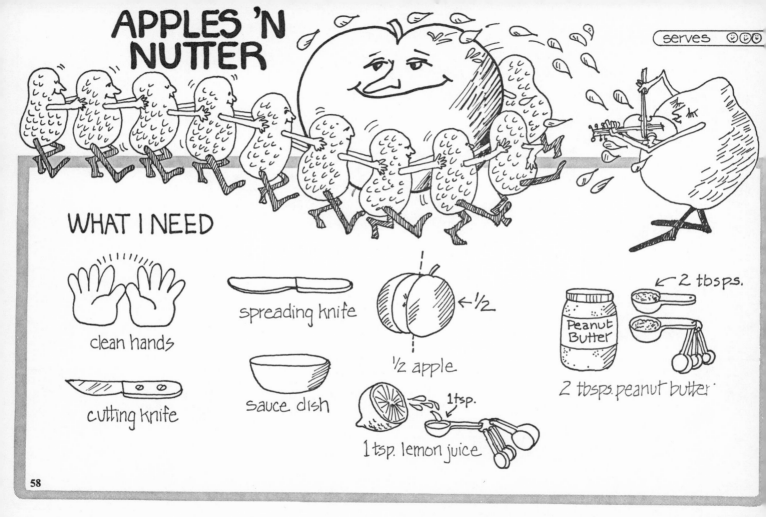

WHAT I NEED

clean hands

cutting knife

spreading knife

sauce dish

½ apple ←½

1 tsp. lemon juice ←1 tsp.

Peanut Butter

2 tbsps. peanut butter ←2 tbsps.

58

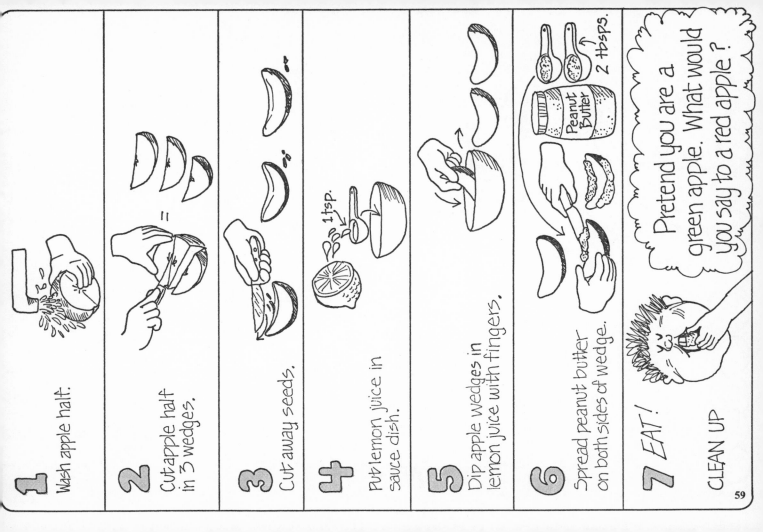

1 Wash apple half.

2 Cut apple half in 3 wedges.

3 Cut away seeds.

4 Put lemon juice in sauce dish. 1 tsp.

5 Dip apple wedges in lemon juice with fingers.

6 Spread peanut butter on both sides of wedge. Peanut Butter 2 tbsps.

7 EAT!

CLEAN UP

Pretend you are a green apple. What would you say to a red apple?

59

FRUIT NIBBLES

serves

WHAT I NEED

FRUIT IN SEASON

clean hands

peeler

toothpicks

cutting knife

sauce dish

1 tbsp. lemon juice

1 tbsp.

tray

① Wash fruit.

② Peel fruit.

③ Take out seeds.

④ Cut into 1 inch pieces.

⑤ Dip peaches and bananas in lemon juice to prevent browning.

1 tbsp.

⑥ Arrange fruit on tray.

⑦ Get into a circle.

⑧ Pass tray with toothpicks.

⑨ Stab and eat.

CLEAN UP

☆ Look at each fruit.
☆ Tell how the fruits smelled, tasted and felt.

61

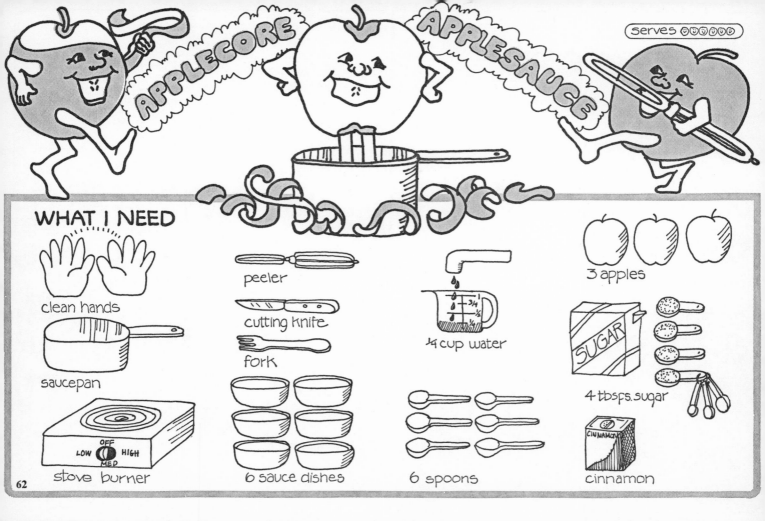

APPLECORE APPLESAUCE

serves

WHAT I NEED

clean hands

saucepan

stove burner

peeler

cutting knife

fork

6 sauce dishes

¼ cup water

6 spoons

3 apples

SUGAR

4 tbsps. sugar

CINNAMON

cinnamon

serves 😊😊😊😊

Stuffed Celery

WHAT I NEED

clean hands

cutting knife

spreading knife

1 celery stalk

Cheese Spread — spreading cheese

water

1. Wash celery.

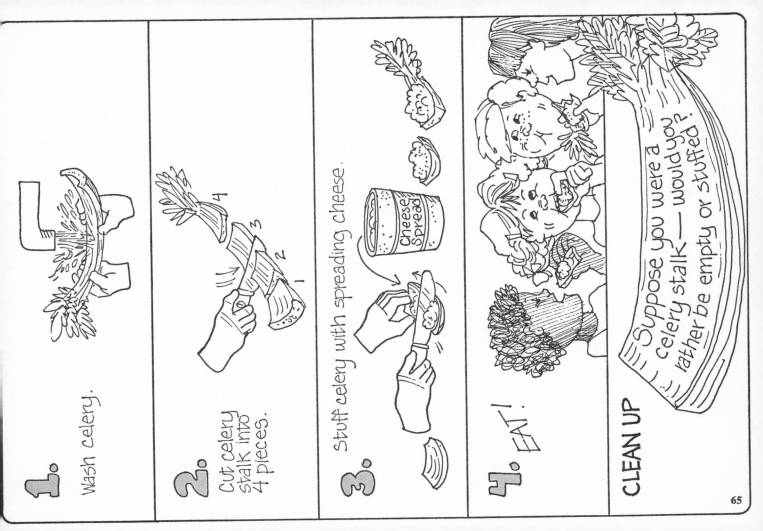

2. Cut celery stalk into 4 pieces.

3. Stuff celery with spreading cheese.

4. EAT!

CLEAN UP

Suppose you were a celery stalk — would you rather be empty or stuffed?

65

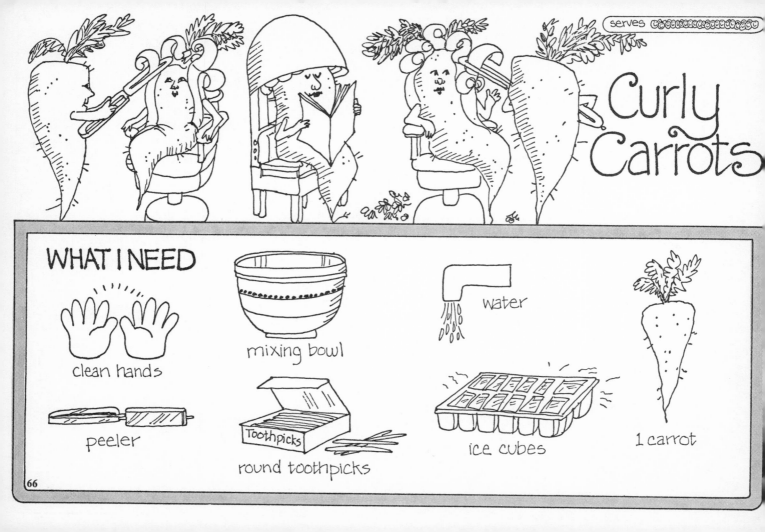

serves

Curly Carrots

WHAT I NEED

clean hands

mixing bowl

water

peeler

Toothpicks

round toothpicks

ice cubes

1 carrot

① Wash carrot.

② Cut off top and end.

③ Peel thin slices with peeler.

④ Roll up and put toothpicks through carrot slices.

toothpicks

⑤ Put water, ice and carrot rolls in bowl.

⑥ Set aside for 2 hours.

2 hrs.

⑦ Take carrot rolls out of water. Remove toothpicks.

⑧ EAT! CLEAN UP

Crunch!

How would you feel in ice water for 2 hours?

67

Raw Vegetable Tastees

WHAT I NEED

clean hands

water

spoon

tray

small mixing bowl

cutting knife

Curry powder

¼ tsp. curry

Mayonnaise

½ cup mayonnaise

½ c.

vegetables

68

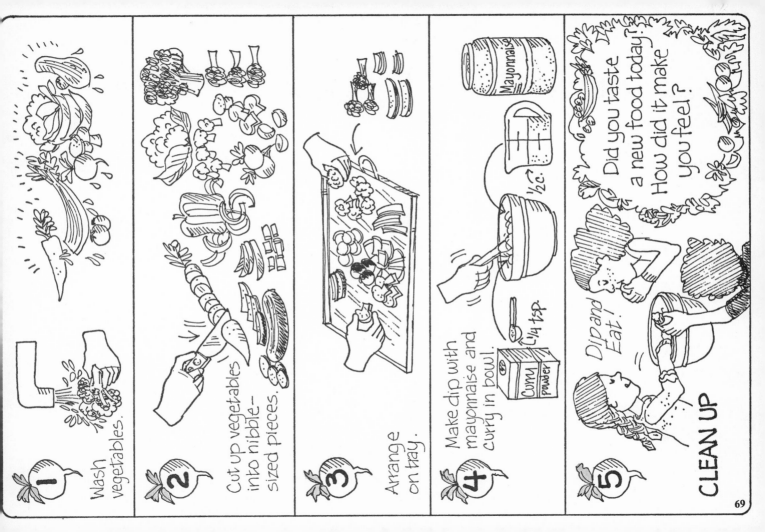

1. Wash vegetables.

2. Cut up vegetables into nibble-sized pieces.

3. Arrange on tray.

4. Make dip with mayonnaise and curry in bowl.

Mayonnaise

½ c.

¼ tsp

Curry Powder

5. Dip and Eat!

Did you taste a new food today? How did it make you feel?

CLEAN UP

69

BRAN MUFFINS

WHAT I NEED

Clean hands

1 1/4 cup flour

3 tsp. baking powder

1/2 tsp. salt

1 cup bran

1/3 cup sugar

1/4 cup vegetable oil

1 egg

spoon

1 cup milk

butter

honey

sifter

paper muffin cups

egg beater

2 mixing bowls

muffin pan for 12

oven

measuring cup

measuring spoons

70

1 Turn oven to 400°

2 Sift the flour with a sifter

3 Combine flour, sugar, salt and baking powder in mixing bowl

SALT   ½ tsp.   BAKING POWDER   3 tsp.   SUGAR

4 Combine milk and bran in bowl

MILK   BRAN

5 Add egg and oil. Beat vigorously

vegetable OIL   ¼

6 Put flour mixture into the milk mixture.... stir.

7 Put paper cups in muffin pan

8 Fill paper cups ⅔ full

9 Bake 25 minutes...turn off oven...cool muffins

OFF

10 EAT — with butter and honey

HONEY

CLEAN UP

Invite someone to observe while you cook and then to eat with you.

71

Old-Fashioned Biscuits

serves

WHAT I NEED

clean hands

measuring spoons

bread board

2 cups flour, plus flour for board

←1c. + ←1c. +½

½ tsp. salt

bowl

measuring cup

cookie sheet

←½ c.

½ cup shortening

fork

biscuit cutter

oven

3 tsps. baking powder

←1 tsp. + 1 tsp. + 1 tsp.

⅔ cup milk

←⅔ c.

72

1. Set oven to 425°.

425°

2. Put flour, baking powder and salt in bowl.

FLOUR
1 c. + 1 c.
BAKING POWDER
1 tsp.
1 tsp.
1 tsp.
SALT
½ tsp.

3. Add shortening. Cut in with fork.

shortening
½ c.

4. Add milk and mix with fork.

MILK
2/3 c.

5. Spread flour on bread board.

FLOUR

6. Knead dough on floured board.

7. Pat out dough to ½" thick. Cut with biscuit cutter.

8. Place on cookie sheet. Bake for 15 minutes.

15 minutes
OFF

9. EAT! CLEAN UP Kneading is like.....

73

Jack·O·Lantern Bread

WHAT I NEED

clean hands

2 mixing bowls

cooking spoon

bread knife

cake rack

loaf pan 9"x5"

oven

egg beater   paper towels

1 2/3 cups flour

1/4 tsp. baking powder

1 tsp. baking soda

3/4 tsp. salt

2 eggs

1/2 tsp. cinnamon

1/2 tsp. nutmeg

1 1/3 cups sugar

1/2 cup chopped walnuts

1/2 cup oil, plus oil to grease pan

1/2 tsp. vanilla

1 cup canned pumpkin

1/3 cup water

74

1 350°

Turn oven to 350°.

2 Grease loaf pan. (Use paper towel to grease pan.)

3 ⌐1/4 tsp. Salt ⌐1/2 tsp.

1c. FLOUR 2/3 c.

⌐1/2 tsp. Cinnamon

⌐1/2 tsp. NUTMEG

BAKING POWDER ⌐1/4 tsp.

BAKING SODA ⌐1 tsp.

1c.

SUGAR

1/3c. 1/2c.

Put flour, baking powder, baking soda, salt, cinnamon, nutmeg, sugar and walnuts in bowl.

4 Mix.

5 1/2 c. Vegetable OIL

⌐1/2 tsp. Vanilla 1c. pkin

←1/3 c.

Put into other bowl, oil, vanilla, eggs, pumpkin and water.

6 Beat liquids with egg beater.

7 Pour pumpkin mixture into flour mixture. Mix.

8 Pour mixture into loaf pan.

9 50 minutes

OFF

Bake 50 minutes. Turn oven off.

10 Cool on cake rack.

11 Slice. EAT!

CLEAN UP

Think about it... What is your favorite bread?

75

CRISP CHICKEN DRUMS

WHAT I NEED

clean hands

plastic bag (small)

oven

corn flakes

¼ cup milk

rolling pin

shallow baking dish

napkins

measuring cup

¼ tsp. pepper

wax paper

bowl

6 chicken legs (rinse)

¼ tsp. paprika

¼ tsp. salt

76

1 Set oven at 375°

375°

2 Crush corn flakes to make ½ cup. Combine with paprika, pepper and salt in plastic bag.

SALT

F ¼ tsp.

PEPPER

¼ tsp.

Paprika

¼ tsp.

CORN FLAKES

WAX PAPER

½ c

3 Put milk in bowl, dip in chicken.

MILK

¼ c.

4 Shake chicken in bag with corn flakes.

5 Place chicken in baking dish.

6 Bake 50 minutes.

50 min.

7 CLEAN UP

EAT!

Create or tap out a crisp rhythm!

77

serves

CAN CAN CASSEROLE

WHAT I NEED

clean hands

can opener

baking dish — 13" · 9" · 2"

wooden spoon

paper plates

forks

grater

oven

cheese

15 oz. TAMALES — 1 15 oz. can tamales

15 oz. Chili Con Carne with Beans — 1 15 oz. can chili con carne with beans

15 oz. CORN — 1 15 oz. can corn

15 oz. Pitted OLIVES ripe — 1 15 oz. can ripe olives – pitted

15 oz. ENCHILADAS — 1 15 oz. can enchiladas

1 350° Set oven at 350°.

2 Open cans and empty into baking dish.

TAMALES
Chili con Carne with Beans
Pitted OLIVES ripe
CORN

3 Grate cheese.

Sprinkle over casserole.

4 Bake 35 minutes.
35 min.

5 Serve and eat!

CLEAN UP

When you do things with other people, what do you like to do best in the whole world?

79

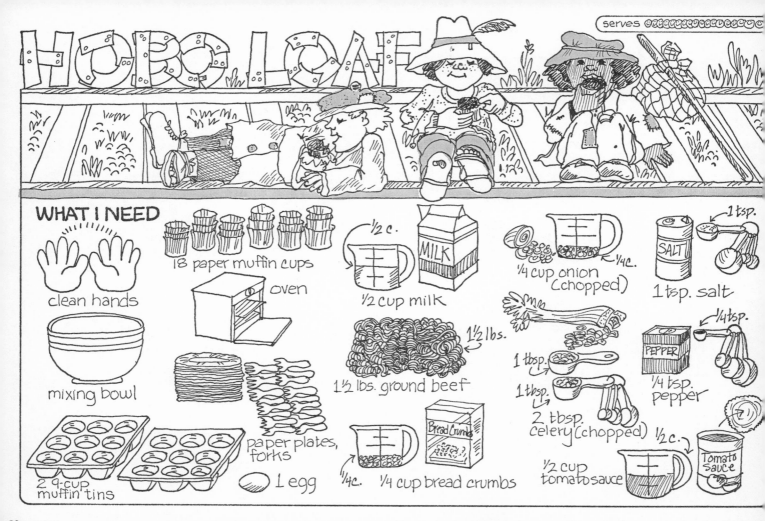

HOBO LOAF

serves

WHAT I NEED

clean hands

mixing bowl

2 9-cup muffin tins

18 paper muffin cups

oven

paper plates, forks

1 egg

½ c.

½ cup milk

MILK

1½ lbs. ground beef

¼ c.

¼ cup bread crumbs

Bread Crumbs

¼ cup onion (chopped)

1 tbsp.

1 tbsp.

2 tbsp. celery (chopped)

½ cup tomato sauce

Tomato Sauce

SALT

1 tsp.

1 tsp. salt

PEPPER

¼ tsp.

¼ tsp. pepper

1 350°
Set oven at 350°.

2 Put paper muffin cups in muffin tin.

3 Combine all ingredients in bowl.
SALT 1 tsp.
1 tbsp. ← 1 tbsp.
1½ lbs. 2
Tomato Sauce
½ c.
PEPPER ← 1/4 tsp.
MILK
½ c.
Bread Crumb
¼ c.
¼ c.

4 Mix with hands.

5 Put 1 handful of mixture in each cup. (About ¼ cup.)
not full

6 Bake 45 minutes.
10 11 12 1 2 3 ← 45 min.
9 8 7 6 5 4

7 EAT! ..... CLEAN UP.
When you feel like loafing, what do you do?

81

The All Together Stew

WHAT I NEED

clean hands

stove burner

plastic bag

bowls

cooking pot

spoons

wooden spoon

ladle

oil for pot

2 lbs. chopped stew meat

1 cup flour

1/2 tsp. salt

1/4 tsp. pepper

stew seasoning

6 potatoes (diced)

6 carrots (diced)

8 oz. 18oz. can peas

28 oz. 1 large can tomatoes

3 cups and 1/4 cup water

3 tbsp. corn starch

1 onion — chopped

82

1. Turn stove to high. Add oil to cover bottom of pot. Heat.

2. Put flour, salt and pepper in bag.

3. Put meat in bag. Shake.

4. Brown onions and stew meat.

5. Add 3 cups water, tomatoes and stew meat seasoning.

6. Put on lid and reduce heat. Simmer 1 hr.

7. Add vegetables. Simmer ½ hr.

8. Mix ¼ cup water and corn starch. Add to stew. Stir until thick.

9. Serve and EAT! CLEAN UP. How do you feel when you are all stewed up?

83

All-American Barbecue Beans

☆☆☆☆☆☆☆

WHAT I NEED

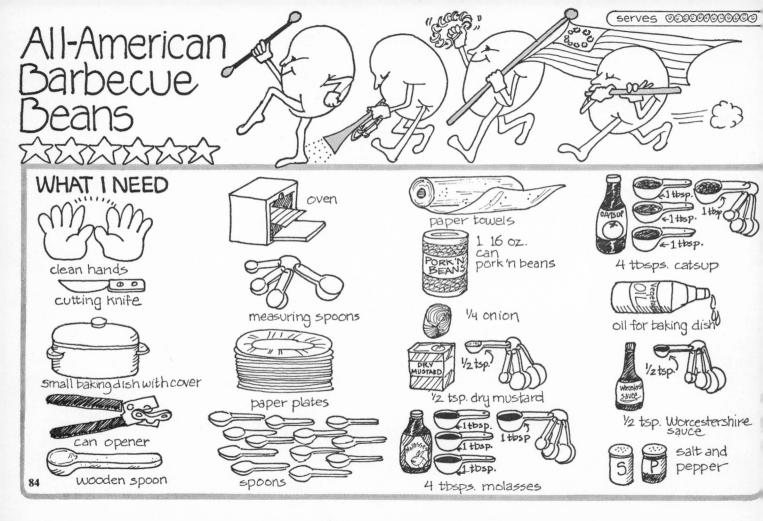

clean hands

cutting knife

small baking dish with cover

can opener

wooden spoon

oven

measuring spoons

paper plates

spoons

paper towels

1 16 oz. can pork 'n beans

PORK 'N BEANS

¼ onion

DRY MUSTARD   ½ tsp.

½ tsp. dry mustard

←1 tbsp.
←1 tbsp.   1 tbsp.
←1 tbsp.

Molasses

4 tbsps. molasses

CATSUP   ←1 tbsp.
          ←1 tbsp.   1 tbsp.
          ←1 tbsp.

4 tbsps. catsup

Vegetable OIL

oil for baking dish

Worcestershire sauce   ½ tsp.

½ tsp. Worcestershire sauce

S   P

salt and pepper

84

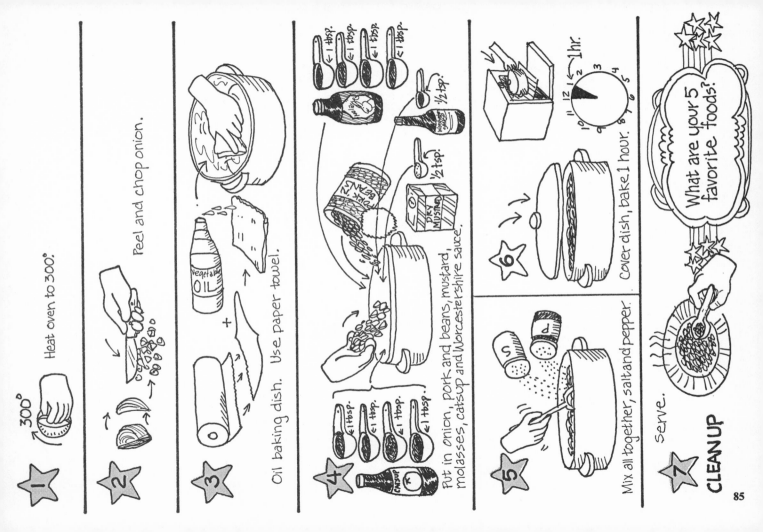

★ 1 300° Heat oven to 300°.

★ 2 Peel and chop onion.

★ 3 Oil baking dish. Use paper towel.

★ 4 1 tbsp. 1 tbsp. 1 tbsp. 1 tbsp. ½ tsp. ½ tsp. 1 tbsp. 1 tbsp. 1 tbsp. 1 tbsp.
Put in onion, pork and beans, mustard, molasses, catsup and Worcestershire sauce.

★ 5 Mix all together, salt and pepper. Cover dish, bake 1 hour.

★ 6

★ 7 Serve. CLEANUP

What are your 5 favorite "foods"?

85

SOUL GREENS

WHAT I NEED

Clean hands

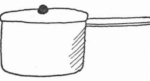

large pan

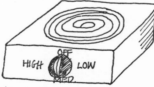

colander

stove burner

paper plates

forks

cutting knife

bacon bits

butter

2 strips bacon

SALT PEPPER

salt and pepper

fresh or frozen
spinach

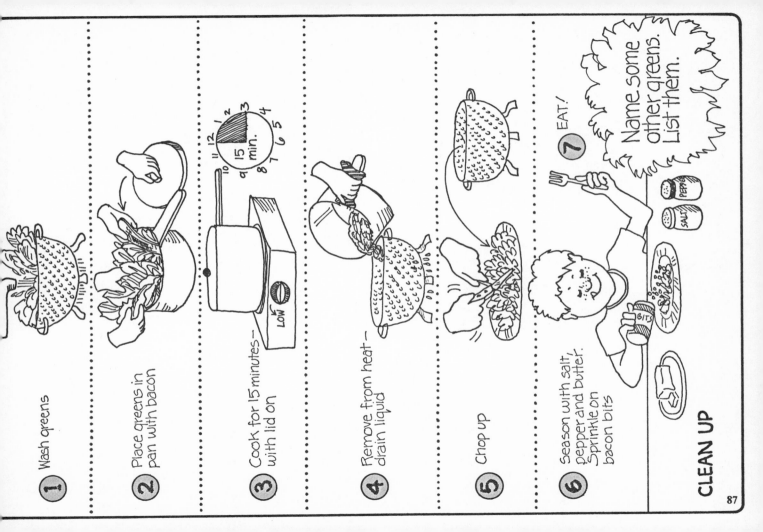

1. Wash greens

2. Place greens in pan with bacon

3. Cook for 15 minutes— with lid on

15 min. LOW

4. Remove from heat— drain liquid

5. Chop up

6. Season with salt, pepper and butter. Sprinkle on bacon bits

7. EAT!

Name some other greens. List them.

SALT PEPPER BITS

CLEAN UP

87

Oriental Rice and Sauce

WHAT I NEED

clean hands

large saucepan with lid

8 spoons

2 tbsps. butter

✓ 1 tbsp.

+ ✓ 1 tbsp.

wooden spoon

can opener

Chicky Rice

1 package prepared rice mix

small saucepan

8 sauce dishes

1 c.

1 c. + 1/2 c.

2 1/2 cups water

SWEET 'N SOUR SAUCE — 1/2

1/2 16 oz. can Sweet and Sour Sauce

88 stove burner

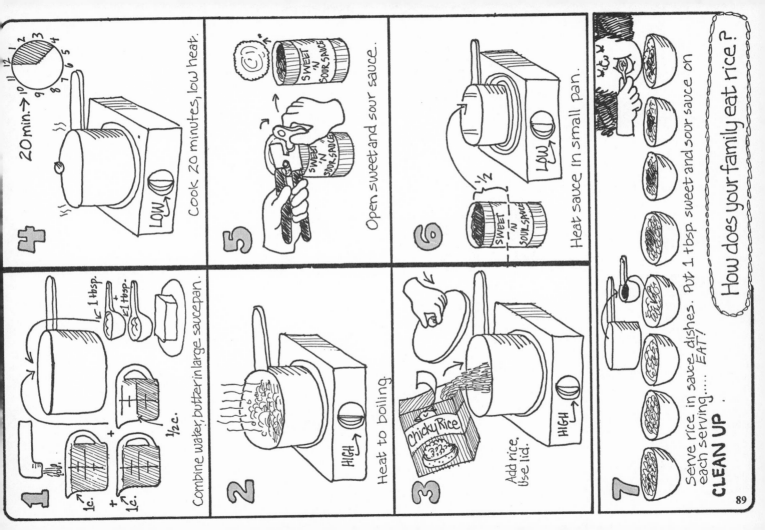

4

20 min. →

Cook 20 minutes, low heat.

LOW

5

SWEET 'N SOUR SAUCE

Open sweet and sour sauce.

6

½

SWEET 'N SOUR SAUCE

LOW

Heat sauce in small pan.

1

1 tbsp.

1 tbsp.

½ c.

1 c.

1 c.

Combine water, butter in large saucepan.

2

HIGH

Heat to boiling.

3

Chicky Rice

HIGH

Add rice, use lid.

7

Serve rice in sauce dishes. Put 1 tbsp sweet and sour sauce on each serving...... EAT!
CLEAN UP .

How does your family eat rice?

serves 〇〇〇〇〇〇〇〇〇〇〇〇

TACO TACO

WHAT I NEED

clean hands

napkins

salt and pepper

grated cheese

stove burner

paper plates

12 TACO SHELLS

1 package taco shells

shredded lettuce

wooden spoon

5 sauce dishes.

Vegetable OIL

1 tbsp.

1 tbsp. oil

½ lb. hamburger

chopped onion

diced tomatoes

TACO SAUCE

taco sauce

frying pan

90

FILLING

1 Put hamburger in frying pan. Break into bits.

2 Turn heat to medium under pan. Brown meat. Stir. Salt and pepper.

3 OFF — Turn off stove.

4 Put hamburger in sauce dish.

TACO

1 Place frying pan on medium heat. Put 1 tbsp. oil in pan.

MED.

OIL — 1 tbsp.

2 Heat taco shell on both sides.

12 TACO SH—

MED   MED   MED

Set up a taco line

Heat taco, add: meat, onions, cheese, lettuce, tomatoes, and taco sauce. EAT!

What did it feel like to work in a taco line?

CLEAN UP

91

Italian Spaghetti

serves

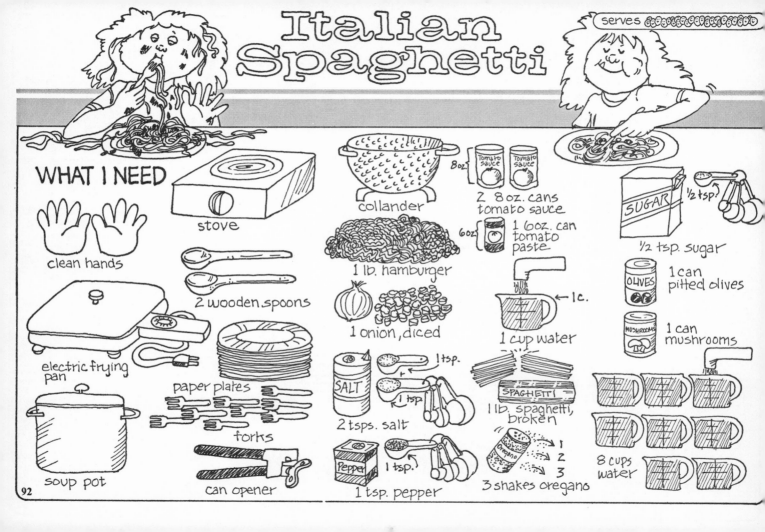

WHAT I NEED

- clean hands
- stove
- 2 wooden spoons
- electric frying pan
- paper plates
- forks
- soup pot
- can opener

- collander
- 1 lb. hamburger
- 1 onion, diced
- 2 tsps. salt
- 1 tsp. pepper

- 2 8 oz. cans tomato sauce
- 1 6 oz. can tomato paste
- 1 cup water
- 1 lb. spaghetti, broken
- 3 shakes oregano

- ½ tsp. sugar
- 1 can pitted olives
- 1 can mushrooms
- 8 cups water

92

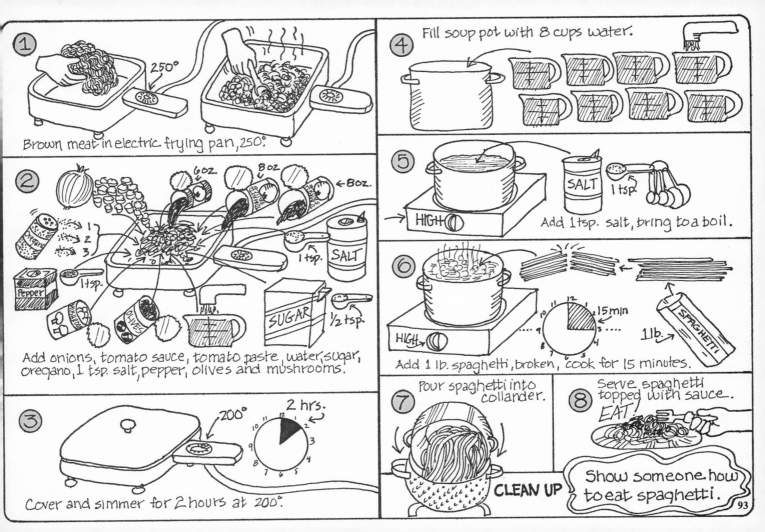

1. Brown meat in electric frying pan, 250°.
250°

2. 6 oz. 8 oz. ←8 oz.
1 2 3
Oregano
Pepper 1 tsp.
OLIVES
SALT 1 tsp.
SUGAR ½ tsp.
Add onions, tomato sauce, tomato paste, water, sugar, oregano, 1 tsp. salt, pepper, olives and mushrooms.

3. 200° 2 hrs.
Cover and simmer for 2 hours at 200°.

4. Fill soup pot with 8 cups water.

5. SALT 1 tsp. HIGH
Add 1 tsp. salt, bring to a boil.

6. HIGH 15 min 1 lb. SPAGHETTI
Add 1 lb. spaghetti, broken, cook for 15 minutes.

7. Pour spaghetti into collander.
CLEAN UP

8. Serve spaghetti topped with sauce. EAT!
Show someone how to eat spaghetti.

93

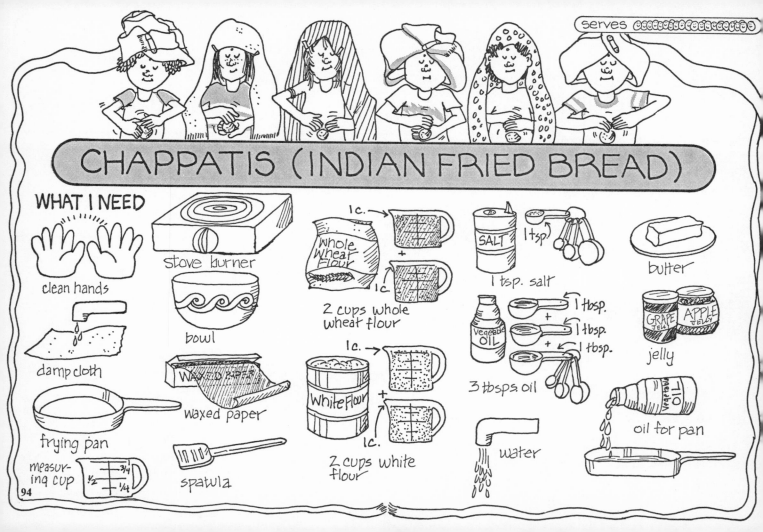

CHAPPATIS (INDIAN FRIED BREAD)

WHAT I NEED

clean hands

stove burner

bowl

damp cloth

WAXED PAPER — waxed paper

frying pan

measuring cup

spatula

2 cups whole wheat flour

2 cups white flour

1 tsp. salt

3 tbsps. oil

water

butter

jelly

oil for pan

94

1. Mix flour and salt, 3 tbsps. oil together and add enough water to make soft dough.

2. Break into small balls for each person.

3. Knead 10 minutes on waxed paper.

4. Cover with damp cloth, let rise 1 hour.

5. Break into large marble size balls.

6. Roll and pat flat on waxed paper.

7. Heat oil in frying pan over medium heat.

8. Fry a few pieces at a time.

9. CLEAN UP

Serve warm with butter and jelly.

Would you like to be from India?

95

POPCORN FIREWORKS

Serves

WHAT I NEED

clean hands

popcorn popper

large plastic cover

small brown bags

1/3 cup colored popcorn

1 tsp. butter

2 Tbsp. oil

SALT

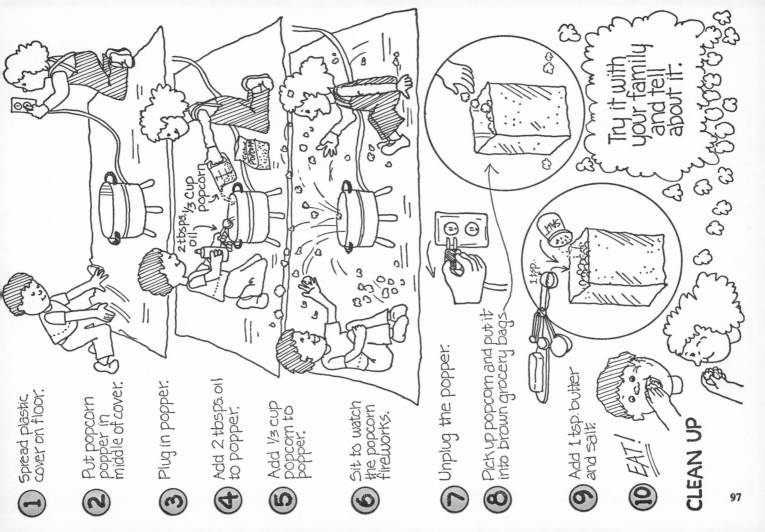

1. Spread plastic cover on floor.

2. Put popcorn popper in middle of cover.

3. Plug in popper.

4. Add 2 tbsps. oil to popper.

5. Add 1/3 cup popcorn to popper.

6. Sit to watch the popcorn fireworks.

7. Unplug the popper.

8. Pick up popcorn and put it into brown grocery bags.

9. Add 1 tsp. butter and salt.

10. *EAT!*

CLEAN UP

2 tbsps. 1/3 cup oil popcorn

1 tsp.

Try it with your family and tell about it.

SWIMMERS, DIVERS, and MYSTERY GUESTS

WHAT I NEED

clean hands

saucepan

refrigerator

large mixing bowl

spoons

stove burner

paper plates

wooden spoon

cutting knife

glass loaf pan (9"x13"x2")

2 6oz. packages flavored gelatin

4 cups water

4 cups fruit juice

1. Heat water to boiling.

2. Pour water and gelatin into mixing bowl. Stir.

3. Pour gelatin mixture into loaf dish. Add fruit juice.

4. Prepare nibble-sized vegetables and fruits brought from home.

5. Drop vegetables and fruits into gelatin mixture. Examine for swimmers and divers.

6. Refrigerate overnight.

CLEAN UP

7. Cut into squares.

EAT!

What food did you add to the gelatin?

99

It Won't Melt Jell

WHAT I NEED

clean hands

stove burner

refrigerator

wooden spoon

shallow pan, 9"x13"x2"

saucepan

cutting knife

4 packages unflavored gelatin

4 cups water

1c.   1c.

1c.   1c.

3 3oz. packages flavored gelatin

3oz.

1 cup cold fruit juice

FRUIT JUICE

1 cup

SUGAR

½ cup sugar

½ cup

100

1st DAY

1 Put gelatin, fruit juice and sugar in shallow pan.

2 Boil water.

3 Add boiling water to mixture in pan and stir.

4 Refrigerate overnight.

2nd DAY

5 Cut in 1" cubes. Eat with fingers.

CLEAN UP

What is magic about this recipe?

101

Do-It-Yourself Modeling Dough

WHAT I NEED

clean hands

large mixing bowl

large jar peanut butter

powdered milk

wooden spoon

waxed paper (12" square)

¼ tsp. honey

raisins

102

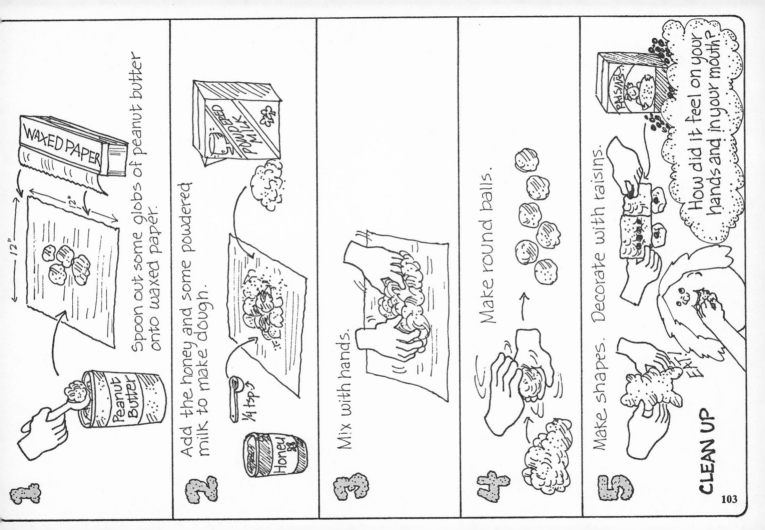

1. Spoon out some globs of peanut butter onto waxed paper.

WAXED PAPER

12"

12"

Peanut Butter

2. Add the honey and some powdered milk to make dough.

CREAM PWDR MILK

¼ tsp

Honey

3. Mix with hands.

4. Make round balls.

5. Make shapes. Decorate with raisins.

How did it feel on your hands and in your mouth?

RAISINS

EAT EAT

CLEAN UP

103

ABOUT THE AUTHORS

Barbara Darpinian is one of the world's beautiful people. Ask any of the kids (young or old) with whom she associates. Barbara is an active curriculum consultant busy teaching, traveling and conducting teacher inservice workshops on current issues such as, "Valuing Education," "Alternatives for Kids," "Community Awareness and School Togetherness." A native of California, Barbara received her education from University of California at Berkeley and Chapman College. Barbara and her family live in Modesto, California.

Em Riggs is known by her friends and home economist colleagues as one who has it all together. Em is a consultant in Health Education and a national lecturer on "The Valuing Process," "I Am a Person," and "The Humanism of Food." She has spent many years working with big and little children to help them understand the basis for nutritious snacks and meals. Em, her husband, two daughters and three dogs live in Sacramento, California.